Sri Chinmoy's

HEART-GARDEN

In celebration of Sri Chinmoy's 40 years

This book is offered in celebration of Sri Chinmoy's tireless efforts to inspire and encourage countless individuals around the world in over 40 years of selfless service to humanity.

Sri Chinmoy's

HEART-GARDEN

A Book of Aphorisms for Joy and Inspiration

Compiled by Sahayak Plowman

NH
NEW
HOLLAND

To my teacher Sri Chinmoy—
you are the silence and peace of the infinite ocean,
you are the vastness and beauty of a thousand
snow-capped summits—you have awakened
my heart and humbled my life.

Gratitude, gratitude,
Sahayak

CONTENTS

FROM THE COMPILER TO THE SEEKER

We are all truly unlimited, if we only dare to try and have faith.
Sri Chinmoy

In 1944, at just 12 years of age, after the passing of his parents, the young aspirant Sri Chinmoy joined his brothers and sisters in the Sri Aurobindo ashram in southern India. Here, for 20 years, Sri Chinmoy studied and pursued his spiritual disciplines of music, prayer, athletics and poetry through silent meditative contemplation.

Internationally acclaimed as one of the foremost spiritual teachers of our era, Sri Chinmoy, now 75 years of age, has unconditionally dedicated his life to the perfection of the human spirit. A keen traveller, Sri Chinmoy energetically offers his teachings to individuals seeking inspiration, hope and encouragement through his meditations, lectures, art, athletics, prose and music.

With more than 100 000 aphorisms in over 1600 books, Sri Chinmoy's wisdom gently raises us above our own limited physical realities, elevating and revealing to us all a realm of higher and all-embracing consciousness.

These hand-picked aphorisms, each echoing like a struck Himalayan bell, offer to the reader the wisdom of eternal and ancient truths infused with modern insights. Allow yourself the time to quietly read and reflect on these ageless teachings; welcome them all, as each carries a clear and loving message. May this be the beginning of a continuing experience of your openness to growth, free from what limits and divides us.

So still your mind, awaken your heart, and embrace these soul-searching truths. May their collective insight be the guiding light to the seeker in you through your life's journey—offering you ever-increasing wisdom, joy, compassion, inspiration and, above all, the capacity to fully realise the beauty and uniqueness of your special contribution to our world.

www.srichinmoybooks.com

www.srichinmoycentre.org

Happiness

May our heart's
Morning happiness
Brighten our entire day.

Try with your heart's smile-power
To change the world.
You will succeed.

Be happy!
Be happy in the morning with what
You have.
Be happy in the evening with what
You are.

If I have just one aim,
And if that aim is to be myself,
Then I am bound to discover joy,
True joy, eternal joy.

True inner joy is self-created.
It does not depend on outer circumstances
Or outer achievements.

Do you want to be happy?
Learn the beautiful art
Of self-encouragement.

There is no magical power
As beautiful, powerful and inspiring
As our smiling eyes.

Just one smile
Immensely increases the beauty
Of the universe.

It is impossible for me to separate
My heart's happiness
From my life's progress.

Happiness is
The heart's great contribution
To life.

My heart's inner happiness
Can easily dispel the heaviness
Of my life's outer burdens.

Do not compare
If you want to be happy.
Do not blame
If you want to be happy.

If you cannot carry
Your inner happiness everywhere,
Your outer life will remain
Terribly unbalanced.

Happiness is not
A matter of chance.
We must cultivate happiness
By virtue of our prayers
And meditations.

Judge nothing
You will be happy.
Forgive everything
You will be happier.
Love everything
You will be the happiest.

Happiness
Is of supreme importance.
When I am really happy,
I have no time
To find fault in others.

*Y*ou are not happy
And you will never be happy
Because you do not lose yourself
Enough to find yourself,
I mean your true self.

*H*appiness
Will follow you
If your heart remains
Undisturbed by trifles.

*Y*ou can be aware of
Your inner progress
By observing the happiness
Inside you.

Happiness is our birthright,
  We just have to believe it.

                    Happiness
          Is our heart's perpetual journey,
            And not a remote destination.

Do you want to know
  Something incredible
  But absolutely true?
The heart of the universe
  Is your soulful smile.

The Heart

Nothing is as beautiful in man
As his heart's sincerity.

Every morning
You must empty your heart
Of endless and useless
Anxieties and worries.

The transformation of life
Begins with a soulful smile
Of the heart.

To brighten your life
    You must
Widen your heart.

Happy is my heart,
Fulfilled is my life,
When I soulfully appreciate
The beauty of creation.

Only the awakened heart
Can see the inner sunlight
Streaming through life.

O seeker,
Bring to the fore
Your inner heart-beauty
And radiate it.

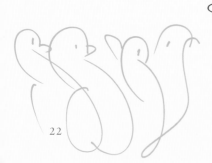

How beautiful to look at
When my prayer
Lights a candle of hope
In my heart.

How beautiful I look
When I live in the daylight
Of my heart's blossoming smiles.

Create a new world
With your heart's sympathy;
You will become perfect.

Be a heart of patience
And a life of dynamism.

Talk and act
Always
From the heart
Of your generosity.

In spite of the advance
Of my earthly years,
Every day
I wish to remain
A child at heart.

My heart is longing for
Simplicity's life
And sincerity's breath.

When two oneness-hearts talk
To each other,
We see the most beautiful dance
Of affection and sweetness.

A heart of silence
Has the capacity
To deepen
The poise of the mind.

The love that the heart
    Cannot trust
    Can never last.

                Our differences disappear
            The moment we come to realise
                That all hearts are one.

    In the morning
    Our hearts open
    To the expanding
    Light of the universe.

I need a simple heart
That gives constant joy
To others.

If you develop harmony with all,
Then yours will be a heart
Totally free from sorrow.

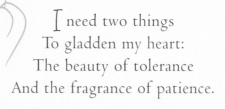

I need two things
To gladden my heart:
The beauty of tolerance
And the fragrance of patience.

Good hearts
Are not hard to find
Provided
Pure lives look for them.

The heart whispers.
Immediately
The world hears.

A heart of inner purity
Is bound to have
A life of outer beauty.

Each soulful thought
Helps the heart soar
With newly blossomed joys.

The heart has a very special way
To see the world
With the help
Of something adorable:
Faith.

If your heart
Does not reach down,
How can your life
Lift any human being
On earth?

The morning light
Feeds our hearts
And guides our lives.

You do not have to broadcast
The beauty and purity of your heart.
Your face can and will
Do it for you.

My heart is all gratitude
To music,
For it keeps me all the time
In tune with my universal self.

With your life
An innocent heart was born.
With your life
A complicated mind will die.

The language of the heart
    Is the only language
That everybody can understand.

    The wisdom of the heart
        Cannot be fooled
        By the clever mind.

        If you are devoted
        To your daring heart,
    Then you are bound to be blessed
        With a liberated life.

The more
The heart can do,
The greater
The life becomes.

The heart-tears
Of every human being
Are so beautiful and precious.

How beautiful a day can be
When we allow
Our compassion-heart
To touch it.

Widen your heart
To include the four corners
Of the globe
In your own life.

Be a true friend
Of your own heart.
Lo and behold,
All will befriend you.

Mine is the heart
That does everything
As whispered by the soul.

I must feel
That my heart
Is a most significant source
Of divine truth.

If you can hold the creation
In your heart,
You will see everything beautiful,
Everything fruitful,
In your inner life and your outer life.

Try to listen
To the dictates of your heart,
And try to establish
Your inseparable oneness
With the rest of the world.

To see
A face of love
Is to feel
A heart of peace.

The sunlit smile
Of your eyes
Comes directly from
The peace
Of your heart.

Unless and until
You have developed
A heart inundated with compassion,
Do not sit
On the seat of judgement.

If you do not find peace
Inside your own heart,
Then you will not find it
Anywhere else on earth.

It is impossible
For my heart
To tolerate anybody
Who cannot admire
The good things in others.

What I need is a heart
That sleeplessly cares.
What I need is a life
That endlessly dares,
And nothing more.

Hope

Hope is sweet.
Hope is illumining.
Hope is fulfilling.
Hope can be everlasting.
Therefore, do not give up hope,
Even in the sunset of your life.

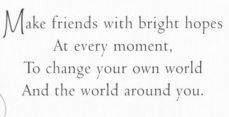

Make friends with bright hopes
At every moment,
To change your own world
And the world around you.

$\mathcal{A}$t the dawn of each day,
Let us make our hopes
And promises
As sincere and powerful
As possible.

$\mathcal{W}$hen I listen to the voice
Of the rising sun,
The beauty of a new hope
Enters into me.

Every day
Our hearts are born
With new hopes.

What is faith?
Faith is the unmistakable
Fulfiller of human hopes.

Every morning, when hope arrives,
I feel that I can become
The possessor of a new life.

The beauty
Of hope's outer life
And the fragrance
Of hope's inner life
Are keeping humanity sane.

Not only every year, every month
And every day,
But also every minute
Abounds with hope.

It is hope
That is keeping us alive
In the muddled mess
Of the world.

Hope
Is the strongest pillar
That protects
The entire world.

To reach our destination,
    Every day we must
    Smooth and pave
    The inner road
With hopes and promises.

No matter what happens,
    Do not lose hope,
    For once hope is gone,
    Everything is gone.

Inspiration

Don't give up!
It is only believing
That keeps us alive
And inspires us to look forward.

Not what happens to you
But how you accept it
Is of paramount importance.

Be brave!
Embrace new challenges.
Your victory will be manifested
In your self-discovery.

When we are propelled
By the power
Of inner faith
We can do the impossible.

You must always accommodate
The birth of
New ideas,
New ideals,
New adventures and
New promises.

There is no such thing
As impossibility!

If you dare to fail,
You are bound
To succeed.

Adversity makes you dynamic.
Adversity endows you
With faith in yourself.

Go beyond, farther beyond!
Do not limit yourself
By comparing yourself with others
Or even with your own self.

Victory
Can never be mine
If I am not willing
To take chances.

What is a challenge,
If not a friend
In disguise
To strengthen us?

Determination and impossibility
Are never to be found
Together.

If we are going to be
Successful in life,
Then we must put all our dreams
Immediately into action.

Yesterday's accomplishments
Are definitely meant
For yesterday only.

You must trust yourself,
Even when the whole world
Doubts you.

Trust not what you hear,
Trust not what you see,
But trust
What you feel.

Think of yourself as a river
Constantly flowing at top speed.
Your mind
Will never be discouraged,
And your heart
Will never be disheartened.

The vision that has
No determination
Cannot be manifested
On earth.

$\mathcal{A}$ bright future is there for us all
If we feel that we are becoming
Younger than yesterday
To embrace new dreams
And new promises.

Determination
Can change your mind.
Determination
Can change your heart.
Determination
Can change your life
Altogether.

We cannot change
The circumstances,
But we can easily stop worrying
Over the inevitable.

We all have the freedom
To build
Our own future.

Avail yourself of every opportunity
That the new day brings,
For every day may not have
Equal possibilities.

If you can believe,
You will definitely know
How to achieve.

I begin by imagining
The impossible
And end by accomplishing
The impossible.

Enthusiasm
Is life's
Most powerful
And most enduring happiness.

If it is difficult for us to identify
With the good qualities of others,
It will be difficult for us to value
Those same good qualities
In ourselves.

Just make tremendous progress
And tremendous improvement
In your own life.
Others will definitely be inspired
By the result.

If your progress in one field
Is obstructed,
Go another way.
Only do not give up
The idea of progress.

Meditations

If your meditation
Is truly high and deep,
Then you are bound to have
A silent dialogue with peace.

Each time I soulfully pray,
A new world unfolds itself,
A new dimension fills me
With astonishment
And I discover startling truths.

When you meditate,
Think of a morning flower
Smiling and smiling,
Radiating its beauty and
Offering its fragrance.
This is how you can make friends
With your soul
And fly with it infinitely higher
Than the confines of the mind.

To create a new universe,
What you need is
The beauty of prayer
And the majesty of meditation
Every day.

My meditation-heart
Is the sole producer
Of my life's excellence.

Each prayer
Is a flight upward.
Each meditation
Is a dive inward.

The more we pray,
The more we are ready
To forgive.

When I want
To say something,
I shall pray.
And when I want
To learn something,
I shall meditate.

Meditation is the only way
To successfully replenish
Our heart-resources.

Meditation is by far
The best encouragement
For a beautiful
And soulful thought.

Remember your highest meditation.
Then with your determination
And eagerness,
Give life to that imagination.

The highest meditation comes
   Through self-giving
   And selfless service
      To the world.

                     I meditate
              So that my mind
           Cannot complicate
                 My life.

          Meditation
     Is of supreme need,
        If silence
     Is our choice.

This morning during my meditation
I had a glimpse of my soul
For the first time.
Never before have I seen
Anything so beautiful.

During my meditation
What do I enjoy?
I enjoy the breath
Of my soul's beauty.

Meditate, meditate!
Faith will definitely be able
To enter into your world.

The stormy life can be braved
Only by the heart's sunny
Meditations.

We are nothing
In comparison to
What we shall become
If we pray and meditate
For the remainder of our lives.

Even before I start
My morning prayers,
I see a stream of blessings
Descending into my heart.

Not by talking, but by praying
And becoming something good,
Can we offer peace to the world.

Meditate silently.
You will be able to create
A totally new life
For yourself.

When it comes to meditation,
Imagine the radiating sun,
And try to radiate like the sun,
Never ceasing, day or night.

When we pray and meditate,
We feel a new life
And hear a new message
With each breath.

The Mind

If you want to expand your mind,
Then every day
Spend as much time as possible
With your heart.

A fool is he
Who thinks that his mind
Is wiser and larger
Than his heart.

Man can be happy and safe
Only when the heart feels faster
Than the mind thinks.

Humanity is divided by
The mind's insanity
And
The heart's sanity.

It matters not how much
Our mind knows.
It matters only how much
Our heart gives.

*A*s your heart
Is meant for deeper things,
Even so, your mind
Is meant for higher things.

*Y*ou are great because
Your mind makes
The right decisions.
You are good because
Your heart executes them
At the right moment.

You will stop hesitating
    When your heart
    Becomes stronger
Than your outer mind.

Your mind's doubts
    Create all problems for you,
    But your heart's faith
Can offer you most adequate solutions.

Reason directs the mind,
  Love feeds the heart.

        The mind wants to see
              And believe.
        The heart wants to feel
        Even without seeing.

      A heart of silence
      Has the capacity
        To deepen
    The poise of the mind.

May my mind's sincerity
Spread like a silver dawn.
May my heart's purity
Radiate like a golden morn.

The mind is
Perplexed
By world-knowledge.
The heart is
Relaxed
Only by inner knowledge.

Stillness of the heart
          Alone
Can cure the illness
     Of the mind.

                    The secret of peace
                    Is to stop the mind
                    From finding fault
                    With the heart.

When the mind's simplicity
     And the heart's purity
          Grow together,
          They create
     Unimaginable beauty.

Difficulties have the capacity
To strengthen your mind.
Therefore,
Do not dislike your difficulties.
Responsibilities have the capacity
To enlighten your heart.
Therefore,
Do not dislike your responsibilities.

We must start our days
With a peaceful mind,
A blissful heart
And
A soulful smile.

The mind's answer
Becomes more complicated
Than the original question.
The heart's answer
Makes the difficult question
Seem very, very simple.

When we live in the mind,
    Everything is uncertain
        And precarious.
    When we live in the heart,
        Everything is optimistic
            And realistic.

                    Not my mind
                    But my heart
                Can play the role
            Of a true peacemaker.

Reflections

A little ripple
Wakes the sea.
A tiny thought
Shakes the world.

*M*ay my everyday life
Be a roaring waterfall
Of creativity.

*J*ust because
We cannot see,
We are not entitled to doubt.

Let us try
To know ourselves!
What we truly are
Is totally different
From what we feel.

Nature's beauty helps us
To be as vast as possible,
As peaceful as possible
And as pure as possible.

I simply do
What many dream of.
I simply do
What others talk about.
I simply become
What others dare not
Even to imagine.

We demand, or at least expect,
Infinitely more perfection in others
Than in ourselves!

Let it be our choice
To make a world
Where everyone
Helps each other.

Let it be our solemn promise
To Mother Earth
That from now on we shall
Take very good care of her.

Wait for tomorrow
To think tomorrow's thoughts.

The moment you know
Who you really are,
All the secrets of the world
Will be an open book to you.

Your outer face
Is bound to show
The pace of your inner life.

If your life does not give joy
To others,
Then how can you expect
Your heart to give any joy
To you.

Not the power
To conquer others
But the power to become
One with others
Is the ultimate power.

Believe in
Forgiving seconds
And not in unforgiving hours.

Inner compassion
And outer tolerance
Can easily make a new world,
A better world.

To forgive others
Is the real blooming
Of our wisdom.
To forgive ourselves
Is the perfect blossoming
Of our wisdom.

Don't be a fool
And assume
That you already know
What you need to know.

The world is ruled
By human opinion.
Even one opinion
Has the strength
To divide the entire world.

Only humility knows
How to appreciate and admire
The good qualities of others.

If we feel inwardly strong,
We will have no need or desire
To speak ill of others.

The first and last
Message of life:
Expect
And you will never get.

Greatness
Is a matter of a moment.
Goodness
Is the work of a lifetime.

Make a sincere effort
To go beyond
What you have already
Received and achieved.

Today
I am determined
To give space
To the unloved ones.

Tell others
When you love them.
This will really make their lives
Worth living.

Don't be discouraged.
As almost every good thought
Had a bad past,
Even so every bad thought
Can have a good future.

Nothing significant
Can come into existence
From mere wishing.

Who says that gentleness
Is not real strength?

Lasting peace must begin
Within the depths of the individual
And from there spread
In ever-widening circles
As a dynamic force
For world change.

Since we take our birth
In perfect harmony,
Can we not depart from this world
In exactly the same way?

If you want to conquer
All your weaknesses,
Then you must face them
One at a time.

If we fearfully cling
To what we have,
We will never be able to discover
Who we truly are.

It is better
To make mistakes
Than to lie idle.

When we encourage others
With no personal motives,
We raise high, very high,
Humanity's progress-standard.

Every second, every minute,
Every day,
Brings new life, new growth,
New opportunity.

Each country's speciality
Must be appreciated and admired
By the entire humanity.

To follow the crowd
Is to miss
The destination.

Walk along the way
Of simplicity and sincerity.
Truth will come to you
And befriend you.

Peace is first
An individual achievement.
Then it grows into
A collective achievement.
Finally it becomes
A universal achievement.

When you work with enthusiasm
You are bound to establish
A free access
To an unending flow of life-energy
And creative power.

Be not self-absorbed.
The world is a member
Of your immediate family.

To help others go
In the right direction,
We must
Go in that direction first.

If readiness,
Willingness and eagerness
Loom large in sincerity,
Then we can accomplish
Everything in life.

The Seeker

Love
Is something
That never cared to learn
How to judge
Anybody.

We must realise
That our inner strength
Is infinitely stronger
Than our outer incidents.

If the modern world had more
Simplicity,
Then the modern world
Would have infinitely more joy
Than it has now.

Each good thought
That you have encouraged
And nourished
Is your life's true work of art.

Whatever you are doing,
If you can feel oneness
With other human beings,
With the world,
Then you will be successful
Far beyond your own imagination.

My life is only half full
   When I receive.
My heart is completely full
   Only when I give.

Every seeker must know
That the best in himself
Will not forever remain buried.
   No, no, no!

Our inner faith
Must determine the line
Of our outer actions.

If you do not expect
  You are, indeed,
    A wise seeker.

Our lives on earth
Last for a few years only,
But
Our hopes and promises on earth
We leave behind to last
Permanently.

I must accept
The responsibility of life,
And not expect
The prosperity of life.

To feel the breath of the universe,
I must remain in tune with my soul
At every moment.

Whom I seek
Is always within me.
What I seek
Is always around me.

There are so many divine things
To see and become
When we go beyond the horizon
Of the known.

Always encourage and inspire
Your fellow travellers
To follow their inner dictates
And abide by their soul's decisions.

If we can all become good citizens
Of the world,
Then the face and fate of the world
Will change overnight.

A leap of faith
Will definitely have
A smooth and safe landing.

The sound of the sea
Inspires me to become
Something great.
The silence of the sea
Aspires in and through me
To make me good.

Be not afraid of death.
See it, take it
And treat it
As a return home.

A true seeker knows the value
Of his inner progress.
His inner progress outshines
His life's outer prosperity.

*I*f your life is ready
To challenge the invisible,
Then your heart will definitely
Be embraced by the unknowable.

*L*ife is a long road.
Along the road at every moment
We must remain cheerful and
Self-offering.

$\mathcal{A}$ genuine seeker
Will definitely be found
Between his life's greatness
And his heart's goodness.

$\mathcal{E}$very second a seeker can start over,
For his life's mistakes
Are initial drafts
And not the final version.

When the mind
Is clear
The dream
Is bright.

Never worry about things
That you are unable to change.
Change your own way
Of looking at truth.

Every seeker
Is bound to find
His inner way home.

To silence enthusiasm
　　At any time
Is absolutely wrong.

There is not a single seeker
Who cannot inspire others.
There is not a single seeker
Who cannot be inspired by others.

The real destination
Is always ahead of us
Not behind.

May my life
Be a total stranger
To all resentments.

Each seeker has to realise
That he is a special
Spark of the Infinite.

We must accept life's
Up and down waves
Smilingly and bravely.

No life should remain
An unexplored reality.

The more we find the truth,
The more we should seek
To arrive
At a higher truth.

The greatest mistake in life
Is to remain indifferent
To the world-situation.

Be not a seeker
In name.
Be a seeker
In action.

Why do you need to search
For outer beauty?
The beauty of your soul's colour
Permeates the entire world.

When you offer something
To anybody,
Do it with both hands
Wide open.

The less we need
From the material world,
The more blessings
We shall receive
From the higher worlds.

First be a member
Of the inner world.
Then become an adventurer
Of the outer world.

Self-giving

A universally
Heart-winning man
Is a breathlessly
Self-giving soul.

*M*ay constant self-giving
Be the guiding principle
Of my life.

*S*elf-giving and joy
Are so fond of each other
That they have become
Inseparable companions.

Willingness knows
That there is no time to delay.
Everything has to be done at once,
Happily and self-givingly.

At morning sunrise
A self-giving heart
Radiates with the beauty
Of the entire creation.

To get happiness
Just look for it in the right place.
The right place,
Is your self-giving heart.

As a tree is known by its fruits,
Even so a seeker is known
By his self-giving capacity.

We all must trust
The infinite power
Of our self-giving life.

Selfless service is definitely
An act of rich creativity.
What have you created?
A feeling of fulfilling oneness
In your life.

My life's self-giving
Is undoubtedly the home
Of all my virtues.

To be sleeplessly self-giving
Is to reach the summit
Of all virtues.

A mother's self-giving heart
Is the child's
All-learning classroom.

Be sincere, be pure, be self-giving!
Otherwise, your accomplishments
        Will never bring
    True fulfilment to your life.

                Every self-giving effort
                Of every human being
                Is needed to change
                The fate of the world.

The sound of the aspiring-heart
　　　Is constant
　　　Self-giving.

　　　　　　　　　　The joy
　　　　　A self-giving heart embodies
　　　　　Can never be matched.

Each self-giving feeling
　　　In our heart
　　Is the celestial radiance
　　Of our soul-beauty.

Self-giving
Is the sacred secret
Of our happiness-life.

I always believe in the capacity
Of my self-giving
In my present life
And not in the achievements
Of my remote future.

First published in Australia in 2005 by
New Holland Publishers (Australia) Pty Ltd
Sydney • Auckland • London • Cape Town

1/66 Gibbes Street Chatswood NSW 2067 Australia
218 Lake Road Northcote Auckland New Zealand
86 Edgware Road London W2 2EA United Kingdom
80 McKenzie Street Cape Town 8001 South Africa

ISBN 9781741102369

Publisher: Fiona Schultz
Editor: Monica Berton
Designer: Jo Buckley
Production Manager: Linda Bottari
Printer: Tien Wah Press (Pte) Ltd, Singapore

10 9 8 7 6 5 4 3

132